MONEY MASTERY: THE ULTIMATE GUIDE TO FINANCIAL SUCCESS

Justin.M.Morrison

Table of contents

INTRODUCTION

Money, if not the most powerful, is definitely one of the most powerful forces in our lives. It affects everything from the choices we make to the opportunities we pursue. But despite its importance, many of us struggle with managing our finances and achieving financial success.

The good news is, mastering your money is not a mystery or a secret reserved for the wealthy few. It's a skill that can be learned and practiced by anyone, regardless of their income or background. That's what this book, Money Mastery: The Ultimate Guide to Financial Success, is all about.

In the following pages, you will discover the tools, strategies, and mindset shifts

necessary to take control of your finances and achieve the financial success you deserve. Whether you're just starting out on your financial journey or looking to take your money management skills to the next level, this book is your roadmap to a life of abundance and prosperity. So buckle up and get ready to embark on an exciting journey towards financial mastery!

FINANCIAL SUCCESS AND WHY IT'S IMPORTANT

Financial success is more than just having a large bank account or a fancy car. It's about having the freedom and security to live the life you want, without constantly worrying about money. It's about being able to pursue your dreams and take risks without the fear of financial ruin.

Financial success is the ability to use your money as a tool to create the life you desire, instead of being a slave to it. It's the power to say yes to opportunities and experiences that enrich your life, and the ability to weather unexpected challenges with grace and ease.

In short, financial success is the key to unlocking the door to a life of true abundance and fulfillment. So whether you're striving to build a successful business, save for retirement, or simply enjoy the fruits of your labor, understanding and mastering your finances is an essential step towards achieving the life you deserve.

THE IMPACT OF MONEY ON OUR LIVES AND HOW IT AFFECTS OUR WELL-BEING

Having discussed financial success, understanding the impact of money in our lives will definitely make you truly value and understand financial success and why they are interrelated.

The topic "Money" is a ubiquitous and often controversial topic that touches every aspect of our lives. It has the power to shape our dreams, aspirations, and life choices. Whether we like it or not, our financial situation can significantly impact our well-being and overall quality of life.

On the one hand, money can provide a sense of security and freedom. It can allow us to pursue our passions, travel the world, or start a business. Having a comfortable level of financial resources can also protect us from unexpected emergencies or financial stress, which can wreak havoc on our mental and physical health.

On the other hand, the lack of money can have devastating effects on our well-being. It can lead to a lack of access to basic necessities like food, shelter, and healthcare.

It can also limit our ability to pursue our dreams or take advantage of opportunities, which can lead to feelings of frustration, hopelessness, and despair.

Money can also affect our relationships with others. It can create feelings of envy, resentment, and power dynamics that can cause rifts in friendships and even family relationships. In many cases, money can be a source of tension and conflict, leading to estranged relationships, broken marriages, and damaged social connections.

In essence, the impact of money on our lives and well-being is complex and multifaceted. It's up to us to understand the role money plays in our lives and strive to create a healthy and balanced relationship with it. By doing so, we can unlock the full potential of our financial resources and create a life of true abundance and fulfillment.

THE PURPOSE OF THE BOOK AND WHAT READERS CAN EXPECT TO LEARN

The purpose of "Money Mastery: The Ultimate Guide to Financial Success" is to empower readers with the knowledge, skills, and mindset necessary to take control of their finances and achieve financial success.

Whether you're struggling to make ends meet, seeking to build wealth, or simply looking to improve your money management skills, this book has something for you.

Readers can expect to learn everything from the basics of budgeting and saving to more advanced concepts like investing and building passive income streams.

But this book isn't just about the technical aspects of money management. It's also about mindset shifts and habits that will help you create a healthy and positive relationship with money.

You'll learn how to overcome limiting beliefs and behaviors that may be holding you back from achieving your financial goals. You'll discover how to cultivate abundance and gratitude in your life, and how to align your money habits with your values and goals.

Throughout the book, you'll find practical tips, real-life examples, and inspiring stories from people who have achieved financial success. You'll also be challenged to reflect on your own relationship with money and take action towards creating a more fulfilling financial future.

In short, "Money Mastery: The Ultimate Guide to Financial Success" is not just a book about money, but a guide to creating a life of abundance, freedom, and fulfillment. So if you're ready to take control of your finances and create the life you desire, then this book is for you.

CHAPTER 1

SETTING FINANCIAL GOALS

Imagine waking up every day with a clear purpose and direction for your finances. No more wandering aimlessly from paycheck to paycheck, wondering where your money went or how you'll ever reach your financial dreams. With a solid set of financial goals, you can create a roadmap to financial success and take control of your money. In this chapter, we'll explore the power of setting financial goals, and how to set realistic and achievable ones that will motivate and inspire you to take action. Get ready to dream big and turn those dreams into reality with the help of this chapter on setting financial goals.

DEFINITION OF FINANCIAL GOALS

Financial goals are like roadmaps that guide us towards the life we want to live. They're a way of putting our money to work for us, rather than the other way around. Just like how we make plans for our careers, relationships, and personal growth, setting financial goals can help us achieve the life of our dreams.

Whether it's paying off debt, saving for a home, starting a business, or planning for retirement, financial goals provide a clear vision of what we want to achieve and help us stay focused and motivated along the way. They're not just about accumulating wealth, but about creating a life of abundance and freedom.

Financial goals can also help us overcome limiting beliefs and behaviors that may be holding us back from achieving our full potential. By setting achievable and meaningful financial goals, we can cultivate a growth mindset and develop habits that will lead to long-term success.

In short, financial goals are a powerful tool for creating the life we desire. They're a way of turning our financial dreams into reality and taking control of our financial future. So whether you're just starting out on your financial journey or looking to take your money management skills to the next level, setting financial goals is an essential step towards achieving the life you deserve.

THE IMPORTANCE OF SETTING FINANCIAL GOALS AND HOW THEY HELP WITH MONEY MANAGEMENT

Setting financial goals is one of the most important steps towards achieving financial success. Financial goals provide a clear roadmap for where you want to go and how to get there. They help you stay focused and motivated, and provide a framework for making smart financial decisions.

One of the key benefits of setting financial goals is that they help with money management. By setting specific, measurable, and achievable goals, you can better track your progress and stay on course towards achieving your objectives. Financial goals help you prioritize your spending, avoid unnecessary expenses, and make informed decisions about where to invest your money.

Financial goals also help you stay motivated and accountable. They give you a sense of purpose and direction, and provide a tangible reminder of what you're working towards. When you achieve your financial goals, you feel a sense of accomplishment and satisfaction, which can fuel your motivation to continue making progress towards your next set of goals.

Additionally, financial goals can help you overcome limiting beliefs and behaviors that may be holding you back from achieving financial success. By setting ambitious but realistic goals, you can cultivate a growth mindset and develop habits that will lead to long-term success.

In summary, setting financial goals is a critical step towards achieving financial success. They help with money management, provide motivation and accountability, and can help you overcome limiting beliefs and behaviors. So if you're looking to take control of your financial future, start by setting meaningful financial goals that will guide you towards the life you desire.

HOW TO SET REALISTIC AND ACHIEVABLE FINANCIAL GOALS.

Now about setting realistic and achievable financial goals, this is crucial for achieving financial success. While it's important to dream big, it's equally important to be practical and realistic about what you can achieve with your resources and abilities. Here are some tips on how to set realistic and achievable financial goals:

Identify your priorities: Start by identifying what's most important to you in your life. Is it owning a home, traveling the world, or retiring comfortably? Once you know your priorities, you can set financial goals that align with your values and aspirations.

Make your goals specific and measurable: A vague goal like "saving more money" is not helpful because it lacks specificity and measurability. Instead, make your goals specific and measurable, such as "saving $10,000 for a down payment on a home within the next 12 months."

Break down larger goals into smaller ones: If your financial goal is a large one, such as retiring comfortably, it can be helpful to break it down into smaller, more manageable goals. For example, you could set a goal of increasing your retirement savings by a certain percentage each year.

Be realistic: When setting financial goals, it's important to be realistic about what you can achieve with your current resources and abilities. Setting a goal that is too ambitious can be discouraging and lead to feelings of failure.

Track your progress: Regularly track your progress towards your financial goals. This will help you stay motivated and make any necessary adjustments along the way.

Remember, setting realistic and achievable financial goals is a process. It takes time, effort, and commitment to achieve financial success. But by following these tips, you'll be well on your way to creating a financial future that aligns with your values and aspirations.

EXAMPLES OF SHORT-TERM AND LONG-TERM FINANCIAL GOALS.

Short-term financial goals are typically achievable within a few months to a year, while long-term financial goals may take several years or even decades to accomplish. Here are some examples of short-term and long-term financial goals:

Short-term Financial Goals:

1. Building an emergency fund with 3-6 months' worth of living expenses.
2. Paying off a credit card or other high-interest debt within the next 6 months.
3. Saving up for a vacation or a down payment on a car within the next year.
4. Investing in a retirement account or a brokerage account to start building wealth.

Long-term Financial Goals:

1. Saving up for a down payment on a house within the next 5 years.
2. Paying off all debt, including a mortgage, within the next 10-15 years.

3. Building a retirement nest egg that will sustain you for the rest of your life.
4. Starting a business or investing in real estate to generate passive income.

NOTE: It's important to remember that financial goals should be specific, measurable, and realistic. So when setting your own financial goals, make sure to consider your current financial situation, your values, and your aspirations for the future.

CHAPTER 2

BUDGETING AND SAVING

Welcome to the chapter on budgeting and saving, where we explore one of the most crucial aspects of financial success. Money management is a skill that requires discipline, focus, and a solid plan. It's not just about earning more money; it's about knowing how to use it wisely. By budgeting and saving, you can take control of your finances and make your money work for you. Whether you're aiming to pay off debt, save for a dream vacation, or plan for retirement, this chapter will provide you with practical tips and strategies to help you achieve your goals. So, let's dive in and learn how to create a budget that fits your lifestyle and start saving for the future you deserve.

THE IMPORTANCE OF CREATING A BUDGET AND HOW TO CREATE ONE.

Creating a budget is just too essential for managing your money effectively and achieving your desired financial success. A budget allows you to track your income and expenses, identify areas where you can cut back or save more, and make informed decisions about how to use your money. So, here are some tips on how to create a budget:

Track your income and expenses: Start by tracking all of your income and expenses for at least a month. This will give you a clear picture of your spending habits and where your money is going.

Categorize your expenses: Once you have a good understanding of your income and expenses, categorize your expenses into different categories such as housing, transportation, food, entertainment, etc.

Determine your fixed and variable expenses: Fixed expenses are expenses that stay the same each month, such as rent or mortgage payments. Variable expenses are expenses that can change from month to month, such as groceries or entertainment.

Set realistic spending limits: Based on your income and expenses, set realistic spending limits for each category. This will help you stay within your budget and avoid overspending.

Review and adjust your budget regularly: Your budget should be a living document that changes as your income and expenses change. Review your budget regularly and make adjustments as needed.

Remember, creating a budget is just the first step. The key to success is sticking to your budget and making adjustments as needed.

By creating a budget and following it consistently, you'll be on your way to achieving your financial goals and living the life you want.

THE DIFFERENT TYPES OF EXPENSES AND HOW TO PRIORITIZE THEM.

Expenses can be categorized in different ways, but generally, they can be classified into two main types: essential and non-essential expenses.

Essential expenses are the costs associated with basic needs, such as housing, food, transportation, utilities, and healthcare. These expenses are necessary to sustain life and maintain a reasonable quality of living. In order to prioritize essential expenses, it's important to ensure that these costs are covered first before allocating money to non-essential expenses. This means that you should prioritize paying for your rent/mortgage, utilities, groceries and even paying off debts before spending money on things like entertainment, dining out, or travel.

Non-essential expenses are the costs that are not essential to daily living, such as entertainment, dining out, travel, hobbies, and other discretionary spending. While these expenses can add value to your life and provide enjoyment, they should be secondary to essential expenses. In order to prioritize non-essential expenses, you can allocate a certain percentage of your income to them once you have covered your essential expenses.

When prioritizing expenses, it's also important to consider your financial goals. By setting specific financial goals, such as paying off debt, building an emergency fund, or saving for retirement, you can prioritize your expenses accordingly. For example, if your goal is to pay off debt, you may need to cut back on non-essential expenses in order to allocate more money towards debt repayment.

Below are a few tactical ways of prioritizing between the essential and non essential expenses

Identify your essential expenses: Start by identifying your essential expenses, such as housing, utilities, food, transportation, and healthcare. These expenses should be given the highest priority in your budget because they are necessary for your basic needs.

Allocate funds for essential expenses: Once you have identified your essential expenses, allocate the necessary funds to cover these costs in your budget. This will help ensure that you have enough money to cover your basic needs.

Determine your non-essential expenses: Identify the non-essential expenses that you can cut back on or eliminate. This includes discretionary spending such as dining out, entertainment, travel, and other luxuries.

Set a budget for non-essential expenses: Once you have identified your non-essential expenses, set a budget for them that is reasonable and fits within your overall financial plan. Be realistic about how much you can afford to spend on these expenses.

Prioritize your financial goals: Finally, prioritize your financial goals, such as paying off debt, building an emergency fund, or saving for retirement. Allocate any remaining funds towards these goals after covering your essential and non-essential expenses.

In summary, prioritizing expenses involves balancing essential and non-essential expenses while considering your financial goals.

By prioritizing essential expenses, allocating a portion of your income towards non-essential expenses, and staying focused on your financial goals, you can manage your expenses effectively and achieve financial success.

TIPS FOR SAVING MONEY AND BUILDING AN EMERGENCY FUND.

Saving money and building an emergency fund are very critical steps to achieving financial stability and security. Here are some tips on how to save money and build an emergency fund:

Create a budget: The first step in saving money is to create a budget that outlines your income and expenses. This will help you identify areas where you can cut back on expenses and free up money for savings.

Set a savings goal: Once you have a budget in place, set a savings goal that is specific, measurable, achievable, relevant, and time-bound (SMART). This will help you stay focused and motivated to save money.

Automate your savings: Make saving automatic by setting up a direct deposit or automatic transfer from your checking account to your savings account. This will help ensure that you save money consistently.

Cut back on expenses: Look for ways to cut back on your expenses, such as eating out less, reducing your cable or cell phone bill, or shopping for deals and discounts.

Use windfalls wisely: If you receive a bonus, tax refund, or other windfall, use it to boost your savings or pay down debt.

Build an emergency fund: Start by setting aside a small amount of money each month towards building an emergency fund. Aim to save at least three to six months' worth of living expenses in a separate savings account.

Avoid unnecessary debt: Avoid taking on unnecessary debt, such as high-interest credit card debt, which can hinder your ability to save money and build an emergency fund.

Stay disciplined: Saving money requires discipline and perseverance. Stay focused on your savings goals and make saving a priority in your budget.

Just know that saving money and building an emergency fund requires a combination of budgeting, goal-setting, automation, expense reduction, and discipline.

By following these tips, you can establish healthy savings habits and achieve financial stability and security.

CHAPTER 3

MANAGING DEBT

Debt can be a burden that weighs heavily on our financial well-being. From credit cards to loans, it can feel overwhelming to manage the many different types of debt we may have accumulated over time. But fear not, because in this chapter we will explore effective strategies for managing debt and reducing the financial stress that it can cause. By taking control of your debt and developing a plan to pay it off, you can regain your financial freedom and move towards a more secure future. So, let's dive in and learn how to tackle debt head-on!

THE DIFFERENT TYPES OF DEBT AND THEIR IMPACT ON FINANCIAL SUCCESS.

Debt is a common financial tool that many people use to achieve their goals. However, not all debts are created equal, and some can have a significant impact on your financial success. Here are the different types of debt and their impact on financial success:

GOOD DEBT: Good debt is debt that is used to finance assets that appreciate in value, such as a home or education. Good debt can help you build wealth over time and can have a positive impact on your financial success. Examples include:

MORTGAGE DEBT: A mortgage is a loan used to finance the purchase of a home. While a mortgage requires monthly payments, owning a home can appreciate in value and provide long-term financial benefits.

STUDENT LOAN DEBT: A student loan is a loan used to pay for education expenses. Investing in education can increase earning potential and can have a positive impact on long-term financial success.

BUSINESS DEBT: Business debt is debt used to finance a business, such as a loan to purchase equipment or inventory. If managed well, a business can generate income and create long-term financial benefits.

BAD DEBT: Bad debt is debt that is used to finance assets that depreciate in value, such as a car or consumer goods. Bad debt can have a negative impact on your financial success and can hinder your ability to build wealth. Here are some examples of bad debts:

Credit card debt: Credit card debt is often used to purchase consumer goods that quickly lose value or do not provide long-term financial benefits. Credit card debt can also carry high-interest rates, which can accumulate quickly and make it difficult to pay off.

Car loans: While a car may be necessary for transportation, financing a car with a loan can lead to negative equity, where the value of the car is less than the amount owed on the loan. Cars also typically lose value over time, making it a depreciating asset.

Payday loans: Payday loans are short-term loans that carry extremely high-interest rates and fees. Payday loans can trap borrowers in a cycle of debt, making it difficult to achieve long-term financial success.

HIGH-INTEREST DEBT: High-interest debt is debt that carries a high-interest rate, such as credit card debt. High-interest debt can be particularly damaging to your financial success because it can accumulate quickly and can be challenging to pay off. Examples include:

Credit card debt: Credit card debt is one of the most common types of high-interest debt, with interest rates often exceeding 20%. It is easy to accumulate credit card debt if you are not careful with your spending, and it can quickly spiral out of control.

Payday loans: As explained before, payday loans are short-term loans that often come with high interest rates and fees, making them a very expensive way to borrow money.

Personal loans: Personal loans can be a good option for people who need to borrow money for a specific purpose, such as home improvements or medical expenses. However, they can also come with high-interest rates, especially if you have a poor credit score.

Car loans: Car loans can also be a type of high-interest debt, especially if you have a poor credit score. Interest rates can vary widely depending on the lender, so it is important to shop around for the best deal.

SECURED DEBT: Secured debt is debt that is backed by collateral, such as a mortgage or car loan. While secured debt can provide access to lower interest rates, it can also put your assets at risk if you are unable to make payments. Examples may include:

Mortgage loan: A mortgage is a loan used to finance the purchase of a home, and the home itself serves as collateral. If the borrower defaults on the loan, the lender can seize the home to recover the debt.

Auto Loan: An auto loan is a loan used to purchase a vehicle, and the vehicle serves as collateral. If the borrower defaults on the loan, the lender can repossess the vehicle to recover the debt.

Secured credit card: A secured credit card is a credit card that requires a cash deposit as collateral. If the borrower fails to make payments, the lender can use the deposit to pay off the debt.

Secured personal loan: A secured personal loan is a loan that is secured by collateral, such as a savings account or other asset. If the borrower defaults on the loan, the lender can seize the collateral to recover the debt.

UNSECURED DEBT: Unsecured debt is debt that is not backed by collateral, such as a house or car. Here are some examples of unsecured debt:

Credit card debt: Credit card debt is one of the most common forms of unsecured debt. It is typically used to pay for everyday expenses and can carry high-interest rates, making it difficult to pay off.

Personal loans: Personal loans are loans that are not secured by collateral. They can be used for a variety of purposes, such as debt consolidation, home repairs, or medical expenses.

Medical bills: Medical bills are expenses that are not covered by insurance and can quickly accumulate into unsecured debt.

Utility bills: Utility bills are services such as electricity, gas, water, and internet that are paid monthly. If not paid on time, they can turn into unsecured debt.

Payday loans: Payday loans are short-term loans that typically carry very high-interest rates and fees. They are often used by people who need cash quickly but may not have access to other forms of credit.

It is important to manage unsecured debt carefully, as it can quickly accumulate and become difficult to pay off.

In summary, the different types of debt can have varying impacts on your financial success. Good debt can help you build wealth, while bad debt can hinder your ability to achieve your financial goals.

High-interest debt can be particularly damaging, and secured debt can put your assets at risk. By understanding the different types of debt and their impact on your financial success, you can make informed decisions about how to use debt to achieve your goals.

HOW TO MANAGE DEBT AND REDUCE INTEREST PAYMENTS.

It is no doubt that sometimes, managing debt can be a challenging task, but there are several strategies that can help reduce interest payments and ultimately pay off debt faster. Here are some tips:

Prioritize high-interest debt: Make a list of all debts, and prioritize paying off the debts with the highest interest rates first. This will reduce the amount of interest you are paying over time.

Consolidate debt: Consider consolidating high-interest debt into a single loan with a lower interest rate. This can make it easier to manage debt and reduce the amount of interest paid over time.

Make more than the minimum payments: Whenever possible, pay more than the minimum payments on loans and credit cards. This will reduce the amount of interest paid over time and help pay off debt faster.

Negotiate lower interest rates: Contact lenders and credit card companies to negotiate lower interest rates. This may be possible if you have a good credit score and a history of on-time payments.

Cut back on expenses: Reduce expenses wherever possible to free up more money to pay off debt. This may mean cutting back on non-essential expenses or finding ways to reduce monthly bills.

TIPS FOR PAYING OFF DEBT FASTER.

Paying off debt is not usually an easy task or responsibility to fulfil, but there are several tips and strategies that can help you pay off debt faster. Here are some tips for you:

Make a budget: Create a budget that outlines all of your income and expenses. This will help you identify areas where you can cut back and free up more money to put towards debt payments.

Create a debt repayment plan: Make a plan to pay off your debts, starting with the debts with the highest interest rates first. You can use the "snowball" method by paying off the smallest debts first and then working your way up to larger debts.

Increase your income: Look for ways to increase your income, such as taking on a part-time job or selling unwanted items. This can help you pay off debt faster.

Use windfalls to pay off debt: Whenever you receive unexpected money, such as a tax refund or bonus, use it to pay off debt instead of spending it on non-essential items.

Consider debt consolidation: Consolidating high-interest debt into a single loan with a lower interest rate can make it easier to manage debt and pay it off faster.

Negotiate with creditors: Contact your creditors to negotiate lower interest rates or to set up a payment plan that works for you.

Remember, paying off debt takes time and patience, but it is worth the effort. By following these tips, you can pay off debt faster and ultimately achieve greater financial freedom and stability.

CHAPTER 4

INVESTING AND BUILDING WEALTH

Having discussed debts in the previous chapter, it's good for us to discuss how we can invest and build wealth with some of these acquired debts or our available capital.

You should know that investing can be a great way to grow your wealth over time, but it's important to understand the different types of investments and their risks and rewards. Here are some examples of investment policies:

Stocks: Investing in stocks can provide high potential returns, but also comes with high risks. Stocks represent ownership in a company, and their value can rise or fall depending on a variety of factors, such as company performance, economic conditions, and global events.

Bonds: Bonds are loans that investors make to companies or governments. They typically offer lower potential returns than stocks, but are also less risky. Bonds can provide a steady stream of income through interest payments.

Real Estate: Investing in real estate can provide both rental income and appreciation in property value over time. However, it can also be a high-risk investment, as it is subject to fluctuations in the housing market.

Mutual funds: Mutual funds are a type of investment that pools money from multiple investors to invest in a diversified portfolio of stocks, bonds, or other securities. They offer lower risk than investing in individual stocks, as they are more diversified, but also provide lower potential returns.

Exchange-traded funds (ETFs): ETFs are similar to mutual funds, but trade like stocks on an exchange. They can provide exposure to a wide range of investments, but also come with risks and fees.

When investing, it's important to diversify your portfolio and understand the risks and rewards associated with each type of investment. By doing so, you can create a well-rounded investment strategy that aligns with your goals and risk tolerance.

Remember, investing always comes with risks, but by doing your research and making informed decisions, you can potentially grow your wealth over time.

HOW TO CREATE AN INVESTMENT PLAN THAT ALIGNS WITH FINANCIAL GOALS

Creating an investment plan that aligns with your financial goals is an important step in achieving financial success. Here are some steps you should follow when creating an investment plan:

Define your financial goals: Start by identifying your short-term and long-term financial goals. This could include saving for a down payment on a house, funding your retirement, or paying for your children's college education. Knowing your financial goals will help you determine the amount of risk you are willing to take and the type of investments that are best suited for you.

Determine your risk tolerance: Understanding your risk tolerance is crucial when creating an investment plan. Your risk tolerance will depend on a variety of factors, such as your age, income, and financial goals. Generally, younger investors can afford to take on more risk, while older investors may want to prioritize preserving their wealth. Use risk tolerance questionnaires or consult with a financial advisor to determine your risk tolerance.

Choose your investments: Once you have identified your financial goals and risk tolerance, it's time to choose your investments. You may want to consider a mix of investments, such as stocks, bonds, and mutual funds, that align with your goals and risk tolerance. It's important to diversify your portfolio to minimize risk.

Determine your asset allocation: Asset allocation refers to the percentage of your portfolio that you allocate to each type of investment. Your asset allocation will depend on your risk tolerance and financial goals. For example, if you have a high risk tolerance and a long-term financial goal, you may want to allocate a higher percentage of your portfolio to stocks.

Monitor your portfolio: Once you have created your investment plan, it's important to monitor your portfolio regularly to ensure that it is performing as expected. You may want to rebalance your portfolio periodically to ensure that your asset allocation is in line with your goals and risk tolerance.

Consider tax implications: Taxes can have a significant impact on your investment returns. It's important to consider the tax implications of your investments when creating your plan. For example, some investments, such as municipal bonds, may offer tax advantages. Consult with a tax professional or financial advisor to determine the best investments for your tax situation.

Determine your investment timeline: Your investment timeline will also impact your investment plan. If you have a short-term financial goal, such as buying a house in the next year or two, you may want to prioritize more conservative investments, such as high-yield savings accounts or CDs. For longer-term goals, such as retirement, you may be able to take on more risk.

Revisit and adjust your plan: Your financial situation and goals may change over time. It's important to revisit your investment plan periodically and make adjustments as necessary. For example, if you have a new financial goal, you may need to adjust your asset allocation or investment timeline.

Don't let emotions guide your investment decisions: It can be easy to let emotions, such as fear or greed, guide your investment decisions. However, it's important to make investment decisions based on logic and analysis, not emotions. Stick to your investment plan, even during market fluctuations, to achieve long-term success.

Diversify your investments: One of the most important principles of investing is diversification. Diversification means spreading your investments across different asset classes, such as stocks, bonds, and real estate, as well as different industries and geographies. This helps to minimize risk and potentially increase returns.

Understand your risk tolerance: Before making any investment decisions, it's important to understand your risk tolerance. This is your ability and willingness to take on risk when investing. If you have a low risk tolerance, you may want to prioritize more conservative investments, such as bonds or cash. If you have a higher risk tolerance, you may be willing to take on more risk in pursuit of higher returns.

Consider the fees associated with investments: Investment fees, such as management fees and trading fees, can eat into your investment returns over time. It's important to understand the fees associated with your investments and consider them when making investment decisions. Look for investments with lower fees, such as index funds or ETFs, to help minimize the impact of fees on your returns.

Monitor your investments: Once you've created your investment plan, it's important to monitor your investments regularly. This can help you identify any issues or opportunities and make adjustments as necessary. However, it's important not to over-monitor your investments, as this can lead to emotional decision-making.

Stay patient: Lastly, after you've created an investment plan, my sincere advice is for you to stay and remain patient. Investing is a long-term game and that's how it is. It's important to stay patient and stick to your investment plan, even during periods of market volatility or underperformance. Over the long-term, a well-diversified investment portfolio can help you achieve your financial goals.

By following these steps, you can create an investment plan that aligns with your financial goals and helps you achieve financial success. Remember to consult with a financial advisor if you need additional guidance or assistance.

TIPS FOR BUILDING WEALTH THROUGH PASSIVE INCOME STREAMS

Passive income streams are a way to earn money without actively working for it. Unlike traditional jobs where you exchange your time and effort for a paycheck, passive income streams are generated by assets that you build over time. These assets can include rental properties, dividend-paying stocks, online courses, or even a blog or YouTube channel that generates income through ads or sponsorships.

The beauty of passive income streams is that they can generate income for you even when you're not actively working. Once you've built an asset that generates passive income, it can continue to produce income for years to come with minimal effort on your part.

Passive income streams can be a powerful tool for achieving financial independence and building wealth over time. By building assets that generate passive income, you can create a steady stream of income that can help you achieve your financial goals and provide financial security for you and your family.

Passive income streams can actually be a great way to build wealth over time. Here are some tips for creating and growing your passive income streams:

Identify your skills and interests: Think about your skills and interests and how they can be leveraged to create passive income streams. For example, if you're good at writing, you could write and self-publish an ebook or create a blog that generates income through ads or affiliate marketing.

Choose the right income streams: There are many different ways to generate passive income, from rental properties to dividend stocks to online courses. Consider your goals, risk tolerance, and available resources to choose the right income streams for you.

Focus on building assets: Passive income streams are created by building assets that generate income over time. This could be a rental property, a dividend-paying stock portfolio, or an online course that continues to sell over time. Focus on building assets that will generate income for years to come.

Start small and scale up: Don't try to create multiple passive income streams all at once. Start with one or two income streams and focus on building them up over time. As you become more comfortable and experienced, you can start to scale up and diversify your income streams.

Stay disciplined and consistent: Building passive income streams takes time and effort. Stay disciplined and consistent in your efforts, even when you don't see immediate results. Consistency and persistence are key to building sustainable passive income streams.

Be patient: Building wealth through passive income streams is a long-term game. It takes time to build assets and generate consistent income. Be patient and stay committed to your goals over the long term.

By following these tips, you can create and grow passive income streams that help you build wealth and achieve financial independence over time.

CHAPTER 5

PROTECTING YOUR FINANCES

Money management isn't just about earning and spending, it's also about protecting what you have worked hard to acquire. In this chapter, we will discuss the importance of protecting your finances and assets through insurance, estate planning, and other essential measures. From unexpected accidents to legal disputes, life is unpredictable, but with the right protections in place, you can ensure your financial stability and peace of mind. Let's dive into the world of financial protection and learn how to safeguard your wealth for the future.

THE IMPORTANCE OF INSURANCE AND ESTATE PLANNING

Insurance and estate planning are crucial components of a comprehensive financial plan. While many people don't like to think about these topics, they are quite essential for protecting yourself, your family, and your assets.

Insurance is important because it helps protect you against unexpected events that can have significant financial consequences. For example, if you're in a car accident and you don't have insurance, you could be facing thousands of dollars in medical bills and property damage. With insurance, you can transfer that risk to an insurance company, which will help cover those expenses.

There are many types of insurance, including health insurance, life insurance, disability insurance, and property and casualty insurance. The type of insurance you need will depend on your individual circumstances and your risk tolerance.

Estate planning is also important because it helps ensure that your assets are distributed according to your wishes after you pass away. Without an estate plan, your assets could be tied up in probate court for months or even years, which can be costly and time-consuming for your loved ones.

An estate plan typically includes a will, a trust, and other documents that outline your wishes for your assets and your medical care. It's important to work with an experienced estate planning attorney to ensure that your estate plan is legally valid and meets your individual needs.

Overall, insurance and estate planning are important tools for protecting yourself and your loved ones and ensuring that your financial plan is comprehensive and effective. By taking the time to understand your insurance and estate planning needs, you can create a financial plan that provides peace of mind and financial security for the future.

THE DIFFERENT TYPES OF INSURANCE AND HOW TO CHOOSE THE RIGHT ONES

Insurance is a crucial part of a comprehensive financial plan. It helps protect you and your loved ones against unexpected events that can have significant financial consequences. However, with so many different types of insurance available, it can be challenging to know which ones are right for you.

The most common types of insurance include: health insurance, life insurance, disability insurance, and property and casualty insurance. So let's take a closer look at each of these types of insurance:

Health Insurance - Health insurance helps cover the costs of medical care, including doctor visits, hospitalizations, and prescription medications. It is essential for anyone who wants to protect themselves and their family against the high costs of medical care.

Life Insurance - Life insurance provides financial protection for your loved ones in the event of your death. It can help cover expenses like funeral costs, outstanding debts, and future expenses like college tuition. Life insurance is an excellent choice for anyone who wants to ensure their loved ones are taken care of after they pass away.

Disability Insurance - Disability insurance provides financial protection if you become disabled and are unable to work. It can help cover expenses like medical bills, mortgage payments, and other living expenses. Disability insurance is an excellent choice for anyone who wants to protect their income and ensure they can continue to support themselves and their family in the event of a disability.

Property and Casualty Insurance - Property and casualty insurance protects your assets, including your home, car, and personal property, against damage or loss. It is essential for anyone who wants to protect their assets and ensure they are covered in the event of an unexpected event like a fire, flood, or theft.

When choosing insurance, it's essential to consider your individual circumstances and your risk tolerance. Consider factors like your age, health, income, and assets to determine which types of insurance are right for you. It's also a good idea to work with an experienced insurance agent who can help you understand your options and choose the policies that meet your needs and budget.

In conclusion, insurance is an essential component of a comprehensive financial plan. By understanding the different types of insurance available and working with an experienced insurance agent, you can choose the policies that provide the protection and peace of mind you need to achieve your financial goals.

TIPS FOR ESTATE PLANNING AND PROTECTING ASSETS

Estate planning is the process of arranging for the transfer of a person's assets after their death. It involves creating a plan that outlines how an individual's assets will be distributed to their beneficiaries, and may include the use of tools such as trusts, wills, and power of attorney.

Here are some tips for effective estate planning and protecting assets:

Make a plan: The first step in effective estate planning is to create a comprehensive plan that outlines your wishes for the distribution of your assets. This plan should include a will, a list of assets, and instructions for the management of any trusts.

Consider a trust: A trust is a legal arrangement that allows you to transfer assets to a trustee, who then manages those assets for the benefit of your beneficiaries. A trust can help you protect your assets and avoid the probate process.

Update your beneficiary designations: Make sure that your beneficiary designations are up to date and reflect your current wishes. This includes designations for life insurance policies, retirement accounts, and any other accounts that allow for a beneficiary designation.

Review your assets: Take the time to review your assets regularly to ensure that they are properly protected. This may include insurance policies, investments, and real estate.

Consider tax implications: Estate planning can have significant tax implications. Consult with a financial advisor or tax professional to ensure that your plan is structured in a tax-efficient manner.

Seek legal advice: Estate planning can be a complex process, and it's important to seek legal advice from an experienced attorney who can guide you through the process and help you protect your assets.

By following these tips, individuals can create an effective estate plan that protects their assets and ensures that their wishes are carried out after their death. This can provide peace of mind and help ensure that their loved ones are taken care of.

CHAPTER 6

MANAGING YOUR MONEY MINDSET

Money is not just a physical currency, it also has a psychological currency that influences our beliefs, values, and attitudes towards it. Our money mindset, or the way we think and feel about money, has a significant impact on our financial decisions and behaviors. It can either empower us to achieve financial success or hold us back from reaching our goals.

 In this chapter, we will explore the power of our money mindset and provide strategies to cultivate a positive and abundant relationship with money. Get ready to shift your perspective and unlock your full potential for financial mastery.

THE IMPORTANCE OF HAVING A HEALTHY MONEY MINDSET

After having said all what has been said in the previous chapters, the power of psychology and strong mentality of course is not a push aside affair in fact it's as vital as the capital and resources in your road map to your financial freedom.

Having a healthy money mindset is crucial for achieving financial success and stability. Our thoughts and beliefs about money can greatly influence our financial decisions and behaviors. If we have a negative mindset towards money, we may be more likely to engage in self-sabotaging financial behaviors, such as overspending or avoiding financial responsibility altogether.

On the other hand, a healthy money mindset can empower us to make wise financial decisions, stay motivated to achieve our financial goals, and overcome financial challenges. It can help us view money as a tool for creating the life we want, rather than a source of stress or anxiety.

Developing a healthy money mindset involves becoming aware of and changing any negative beliefs and behaviors we may have towards money. It also involves adopting positive money habits, such as regularly saving and investing, and practicing gratitude for the financial resources we have.

One of the keys to developing a healthy money mindset is to recognize and challenge any limiting beliefs we may have about money. These beliefs can often be ingrained from childhood and may not be serving us well as adults. For example, some people may have been taught that money is scarce and that they should hold onto it tightly, while others may have been taught that money is evil or that wealthy people are greedy.

It's important to challenge these beliefs and reframe them in a positive light. For example, instead of viewing money as scarce, we can recognize that there is an abundance of money in the world and that we have the ability to attract more of it into our lives through hard work and smart financial decisions. We can also recognize that having more money can allow us to live more fulfilling lives and have a positive impact on others.

Another important aspect of developing a healthy money mindset is to practice self-care and prioritize our financial well-being. This means regularly checking in with ourselves and our financial goals, seeking out financial education and resources, and surrounding ourselves with supportive people who encourage our financial growth.

In addition, developing a healthy money mindset also involves recognizing the importance of giving back and contributing to causes we care about. This can help us shift our focus away from a scarcity mindset and towards one of abundance and generosity.

Ultimately, developing a healthy money mindset is about taking ownership of our financial lives and recognizing that we have the power to create the financial future we desire. By adopting positive money habits and beliefs, we can create a more fulfilling and secure financial future for ourselves and those around us.

COMMON NEGATIVE BELIEFS ABOUT MONEY AND HOW TO OVERCOME THEM

Negative beliefs about money can be a major obstacle to financial success. These beliefs can manifest in many ways, such as feeling like money is evil or that you don't deserve to be wealthy. But the truth is that money is a tool, and how you use it is up to you. Here are some common negative beliefs about money and tips for overcoming them:

"Money is the root of all evil." This is a common misquote of a biblical passage which actually says, "For the love of money is a root of all kinds of evil." The key here is the love of money, not money itself. Money is neutral; it can be used for good or bad purposes. To overcome this belief, remind yourself that money can be a force for good, and that you can use it to make a positive impact in the world.

"I don't deserve to be wealthy." This belief often stems from feelings of low self-worth. It's important to remember that everyone has the potential for financial success, and that it's not about deserving it, but rather about taking the right actions to achieve it. To overcome this belief, focus on developing your skills and knowledge, and take steps towards your financial goals.

"I'll never be able to get ahead financially." This belief can be a self-fulfilling prophecy, as it can lead to a lack of effort and action towards financial goals. To overcome this belief, start by creating a realistic financial plan and taking small steps towards your goals. Celebrate small wins along the way to build momentum and motivation.

"Money is too complicated for me to understand." This belief can be a barrier to financial literacy and can lead to poor financial decisions. To overcome this belief, start by learning the basics of personal finance and gradually building your knowledge. You don't need to become a financial expert overnight, but taking small steps towards understanding your finances can have a big impact in the long run.

By identifying and overcoming negative beliefs about money, you can develop a healthy money mindset and take positive steps towards financial success.

TIPS FOR CULTIVATING A POSITIVE AND ABUNDANT MONEY MINDSET

Practice gratitude: Gratitude is a powerful tool for shifting your mindset. Make it a habit to regularly express gratitude for the money you have and the opportunities it provides.

Focus on abundance: Rather than focusing on scarcity or lack, focus on abundance. Believe that there is enough money in the world for everyone to achieve financial success, and that includes you.

Visualize your financial goals: Visualize yourself achieving your financial goals, and focus on how it will feel to accomplish them. This can help to keep you motivated and on track.

Surround yourself with positivity: Surround yourself with positive people who support your financial goals, and limit your exposure to negativity around money.

Practice self-care: Taking care of yourself, both physically and mentally, is important for cultivating a positive money mindset. Make time for self-care activities that help you feel calm, centered, and empowered.

Educate yourself: The more you know about money and financial management, the more confident and empowered you will feel. Educate yourself about personal finance and seek out resources that can help you improve your financial literacy.

By practicing these tips mentioned, you can cultivate a positive and abundant money mindset that supports your financial success. Remember, your thoughts and beliefs around money have a powerful impact on your financial outcomes, so it's important to cultivate a mindset that supports your goals.

CONCLUSION

THE KEY TAKEAWAYS FROM THE BOOK

1. Financial success starts with setting realistic and achievable financial goals.

2. Creating a budget and prioritizing expenses is crucial for effective money management.

3. Building an emergency fund is essential for financial stability.

4. Understanding the different types of debt and managing them effectively is important for financial success.

5. Investing wisely is key to building wealth.

6. Passive income streams can supplement and eventually replace active income.

7. Insurance and estate planning are essential for protecting assets.

8. A healthy money mindset is crucial for achieving financial success.

9. Overcoming negative beliefs about money and cultivating a positive money mindset is essential for achieving financial success.

10. By implementing the tips and strategies outlined in this book, readers can achieve financial success and security, and ultimately live the life they desire.

A FINAL MESSAGE

Congratulations on finishing "Money Mastery: The Ultimate Guide to Financial Success!" You have taken a significant step towards achieving financial freedom and success. Remember, implementing the strategies and tips you have learned in this book takes time and effort, but the rewards are well worth it. By setting financial goals, creating a budget, managing debt, investing wisely, protecting your assets, and cultivating a positive money mindset, you can achieve financial security and live the life you deserve.

Always remember that financial success is a journey, not a destination. It requires ongoing learning, planning, and adaptation. Use this book as a guide, and continue to educate yourself on personal finance topics. Be patient with yourself and celebrate every small win along the way.

You can do it! With determination, commitment, and the knowledge gained from "Money Mastery: The Ultimate Guide to Financial Success," you have what it takes to take control of your finances and achieve the financial success you desire.

APPENDIX

"It's not about how much money you make, but how much money you keep, how hard it works for you, and how many generations you keep it for." - ***Robert Kiyosaki***

"The individual investor should act consistently as an investor and not as a speculator." - ***Ben Graham***

"In the world of money, which is a world shaped by human behavior, nobody has the foggiest notion of what will happen in the future. Mark that word—nobody." - John **Kenneth Galbraith**

"The stock market is a device for transferring money from the impatient to the patient." - **Warren Buffett**

"Investing should be more like watching paint dry or watching grass grow. If you want excitement, take $800 and go to Las Vegas." - **Paul Samuelson**

"The four most dangerous words in investing are: 'this time it's different.'" - **Sir John Templeton**

"The best investment you can make is in yourself." - **Warren Buffett**

"If you're not willing to own a stock for 10 years, don't even think about owning it for 10 minutes." - **Warren Buffett**

"Rule No.1: Never lose money. Rule No.2: Never forget rule No.1." - **Warren Buffett**

"The secret to success in life is to be ready when opportunity comes." - **Benjamin Disraeli**

"It's not about having more money, it's about having more control over the money you have." - **Suze Orman**

"The habit of saving is itself an education; it fosters every virtue, teaches self-denial, cultivates the sense of order, trains to forethought, and so broadens the mind." - **Thomas T. Munger**

"A penny saved is a penny earned." - **Benjamin Franklin**

"The best time to plant a tree was 20 years ago. The second-best time is now." - **Chinese Proverb.**

"If you buy things you do not need, soon you will have to sell things you need." - **Warren Buffett**

"Financial peace isn't the acquisition of stuff. It's learning to live on less than you make, so you can give money back and have money to invest. You can't win until you do this." - **Dave Ramsey**

"You must gain control over your money or the lack of it will forever control you." - **Dave Ramsey**

"It's not how much money you make, but how much money you keep, how hard it works for you, and how many generations you keep it for." - **Robert Kiyosaki**

"An investment in knowledge pays the best interest." - **Benjamin Franklin**

"The only way to do great work is to love what you do." - **Steve Jobs**

"The best way to predict your future is to create it." - **Peter Drucker**

"Innovation distinguishes between a leader and a follower." - **Steve Jobs**

"Success is not final, failure is not fatal: it is the courage to continue that counts." - **Winston Churchill**

"If you are not willing to risk the usual, you will have to settle for the ordinary." - **Jim Rohn**

"If you want to go fast, go alone. If you want to go far, go together." - **African Proverb**

"It's not about ideas. It's about making ideas happen." - **Scott Belsky**

"I have not failed. I've just found 10,000 ways that won't work." - **Thomas Edison**

"The secret of change is to focus all of your energy, not on fighting the old, but on building the new." - **Socrates**

"If you can dream it, you can do it." - **Walt Disney**

"Your most unhappy customers are your greatest source of learning." - **Bill Gates**

"If you want to succeed, you should strike out on new paths rather than travel the worn paths of accepted success." - **John D. Rockefeller**

"I don't believe in taking right decisions. I take decisions and then make them right." - **Ratan Tata**

"The biggest risk is not taking any risk. In a world that's changing really quickly, the only strategy that is guaranteed to fail is not taking risks." - **Mark Zuckerberg**

"If you want to achieve greatness, stop asking for permission." - **Unknown**

www.ingramcontent.com/pod-product-compliance
Lightning Source LLC
Chambersburg PA
CBHW071139220526

45467CB00015B/1515

9798386612146